June 2000

This resource book is provided by a Cooperative Extension Enhancement Grant. For more information on additional evaluation resources, please call Patty Merk 602-470-8086 X357

HOWARD E. FREEMAN
PETER H. ROSSI
GARY D. SANDEFUR

WORKBOOK FOR EVALUATION

A SYSTEMATIC APPROACH

5

SAGE Publications

International Educational and Professional Publisher
Newbury Park London New Delhi

For information address:

SAGE Publications, Inc.
2455 Teller Road
Thousand Oaks, California 91320
E-mail: order@sagepub.com

SAGE Publications Ltd.
6 Bonhill Street
London EC2A 4PU
United Kingdom

SAGE Publications India Pvt. Ltd.
M-32 Market
Greater Kailash I
New Delhi 110 048 India

Printed in the United States of America

Library of Congress Cataloging-in-Publication Data

Library of Congress Card No. 89-36387

ISBN 0-8039-4459-4

97 98 99 00 01 02 9 8 7 6 5

CONTENTS

ABOUT THIS WORKBOOK

This workbook is intended to be a companion to the fifth edition of Rossi-Freeman. It draws on the experiences of its authors in teaching evaluation courses in a wide range of disciplines and social program areas to students and professionals. From our own teaching experiences, and from discussions with colleagues, we became convinced that the Rossi-Freeman text needed to be supplemented by a workbook. We published the first edition of this workbook in connection with the third edition of Rossi-Freeman. Because the several editions received favorable receptions, this latest edition has been prepared to be in line with the newest, fifth edition.

The very features of the Rossi-Freeman volume that foster its widespread use are also the reasons why the workbook is needed. The Rossi-Freeman text is generally used for one-semester or one-quarter courses, or in workshops which involve even fewer teaching hours. Given the range of material covered in the volume, instructors, including ourselves, find it necessary to move along quite rapidly in order to cover the main topics, let alone all of them. Depending upon students' educational backgrounds and professional experiences, they enter the course with differing degrees of familiarity with the various topics covered in the volume and find some of the chapters are more difficult than others. Thus, particularly for material that a student has not encountered previously, learning can be assisted materially by summaries, reviews and by exercises that can provide rapid feedback to the student and her instructor on the learning accomplished and gaps in knowledge that need to be remedied. This workbook, together with the key concepts that begin each of the chapters in Rossi-Freeman, and the summaries that conclude them should speed up learning the art and craft of evaluation.

Also, the volume includes a fair number of concepts, formulas, and procedures that are new to most persons using the volume in courses and workshops. Learning by putting these concepts and procedures to work should enhance the value of the text and a course in evaluation.

Because there is no substitute for learning by doing, this workbook includes exercises that try to simulate the learning that most effectively takes place by participating in evaluation activities. The design and analysis and reading assignments are intended to extend the educational experience of students, and have been developed keeping in mind the mix of persons who use Rossi-Freeman as a text.

Chapters in the workbook correspond to the titles and content of the chapters in the fifth edition of Rossi-Freeman. Each workbook chapter contains a review of the material presented in the parallel chapter in the text and review questions. Short exercises follow that are designed to highlight the key concepts and important technical material in Rossi-Freeman. Space is left for answers to these sections to be inserted in the workbook. The other two sections included in each chapter--design and analysis assignments, and additional readings--require more lengthy answers, and students are advised to answer them on separate sheets of paper.

This edition contains a new feature—an appendix containing a selective bibliography of evaluations and of important works dealing with evaluation methodology and philosophy, as well as a guide to journals that frequently contain articles relevant to evaluations and to evaluation oriented professional associations. We believe that advanced students who may be interested in pursuing careers in evaluation will find this new feature very useful. The bibliography first appeared in Richard A. Berk and Peter H. Rossi, *Thinking About Evaluation* (Sage Publications, 1990) and is reprinted here with the authors' permission.

We have tried to provide a flexible workbook which instructors can assign in its entirety or from which they can select those exercises and assignments they believe to be especially relevant to their instruction. Because some instructors may wish to review the work of their students (and some even to grade it), the pages have been perforated so that assignments can be turned in and evaluated.

Each revision of the Rossi-Freeman text has benefited from criticisms of professors and students who have used previous editions. We are equally desirous of receiving reactions to this workbook.

CHAPTER 1

Programs, Policies, and Evaluations

REVIEW OF THE CHAPTER

- It is important to remember that evaluation has emerged from both the interests and concerns of social scientists in studying social problems and social programs and from the needs of administrators, planners, and policy-makers in government, foundations, and human service organizations to have systematic ways of operating their programs and deciding upon activities to undertake and to support. [See pp. 27-29 in the text.]

- The design of evaluations must take practical as well as scientific considerations into account. [See pp. 29-33 in the text.]

- One of the practical problems faced by evaluators is that evaluations must be conducted in a continually changing milieu. Features of this milieu include:

    ...changes in the relative influence positions, resources, and priorities of sponsors of social programs.

    ...changes in the interests and influence positions of various stakeholders.

    ...modifications in the priorities and responsibilities of the organizations and agencies implementing programs.

    ...unanticipated problems with the intervention or its delivery.

    ...a lack of a program effect uncovered early in the evaluation.

    ...unanticipated problems with the evaluation design.

    [See pp. 34-46 in the text.]

- Evaluation activities are undertaken for three major reasons:

    ...planning programs.

    ...monitoring program implementation.

    ...assessment of program utility. [See pp. 34-46 in the text.]

• The design of evaluations must take into account what kind of intervention is being considered. The important kinds of interventions include:

...innovative interventions (never tried before).

...proposed modifications in existing programs.

...existing programs [See pp. 41-46 in the text.]

• The design of an evaluation must take into account the purposes for which the results of the evaluation will be used. Evaluations may be intended:

...to influence decision-makers.

...to decide whether or not to implement a program.

...to develop a rationale for action.

...to determine if a program is working.

...to provide the basis for policy or administrative decisions. [See pp. 46-52.]

REVIEW QUESTIONS

1. Give brief definitions of: a. "evaluation research." b. "social program."

2. When did the boom period in evaluation research begin and end?

3. Briefly outline the effects of changes in the prevailing political ideology on evaluation research.

4. Briefly outline the major differences between the approach of Campbell and the approach of Cronbach to evaluation research.

5. What are the three tasks ordinarily undertaken as part of program planning?

(1).

(2).

(3).

6. What are the two tasks ordinarily undertaken as part of program monitoring?

(1).

(2).

7. What are four questions that are often asked in assessing program utility?

(1).

(2).

(3).

(4).

8. How do Rossi and Freeman define an innovative program?

9. What are three reasons for undertaking an evaluation for fine-tuning?

    (1).

    (2).

    (3).

10. What are two reasons for evaluating an established program?

    (1).

    (2).

SHORT EXERCISES

1. Give an example of and describe the delivery system of a social program currently operating in your community, or in your university or college. (If you're not aware of a program in your community or school, make up a program in a sentence or two and then answer the question.)

2. Give an example of the target population of a program in your state.

3. List the categories of major "stakeholders" in relation to the social security system.

4. What three questions would have to be addressed in a comprehensive evaluation of a program to provide medical care for homeless persons operating in about 30% of the communities in your state.

   (1).

   (2).

   (3).

5. Give an historical or current example of:

   (1). An innovative program.

   (2). A modification in an established program that has been or is in the process of being fine-tuned.

DESIGN AND ANALYSIS TASKS [Type or write clearly on separate sheets of paper. If your professor is going to review your work, please make sure you have put your name on each exercise.]

1. Examine the following descriptions of evaluations and identify the reasons for which they were undertaken:

   Evaluation 1: Department of Education Adult Literacy Program:

   For several years the United States Department of Education has funded a program designed to teach illiterate adults to read and write. Thousands of Americans in all parts of the country have participated in this program. Tests have been given regularly to participants in the program at the beginning of their training and at the end of their training to test the level of literacy of each participant. However, no one has examined the results of these tests to determine what effects the program has had on the literacy of the participants. The Department of Education has decided to hire an external evaluator to examine the test results and also to do a follow-up study on participants in the program to determine what effects participation has had on their subsequent work and other life experience. You have been asked by your employer, a private research and consulting firm, to respond to the request for proposals sent out by the Department of Education.

   In what kind of evaluation is the Department of Education interested? What questions might you try to answer if you did the evaluation?

   Evaluation 2: Patient Processing in an Orthodontist's Office:

   An orthodontist in a moderate-sized town is faced with a perplexing problem. He has received several complaints from patients about the amount of time they have to spend waiting in the reception area and about the unpredictability of the length of time they should allot for routine visits. Adjustments of braces and other appliances involve only a few minutes of the orthodontist's or his assistant's time but require a visit by the patient of anywhere from ten minutes to two hours. Further, the reception staff is upset over their inability to control the flow of patients and the hostility they face from impatient clients.

Assume that you have been hired as a consultant by the orthodontist to examine this problem and suggest a solution. What kind of evaluation is called for in this situation? What evaluative questions would you try to answer?

Evaluation 3: Response of an Urban Indian Center to Budget Cuts:

An Indian center in a large city has provided a wide range of services to American Indians who have moved from reservations and other rural areas to the city. These services have included legal aid, employment counseling, emergency food and shelter, and problem assessment and referral to other service delivery organizations. Many of these services were funded in part by a grant from the Administration for Native Americans to the Center. However, this grant has been reduced considerably for the coming fiscal year. With no alternative sources of support available, the Center will be forced to cut back services during the coming year. In order to do this in the best way possible, the Center has asked you to determine two things:

1) What services are most needed by Indians in the city?

2) Which of these services is available from some other source in the city?

What kind of evaluation would this be? What are some questions that you might ask as part of the evaluation?

Evaluation 4: Corrections Legislation Alternatives

A state is concerned about the rising costs involved in incarcerating criminals. One suggestion for reducing these costs is to reduce the number of criminals who are incarcerated and the amount of time they spend "behind bars." One specific piece of legislation that has been proposed for doing this would raise the amount of money involved in qualifying an offense as a felony from $50 to $100. This would apply to such crimes as bogus or "hot" check writing and shoplifting. Opponents of the legislation agree that this would reduce costs for the state government through reducing the number of bogus check writers and shoplifters who serve time in the state system but they believe it would have a detrimental impact on businesses since it might encourage more "hot checks" and shoplifting. The state's Joint Legislative Committee on Corrections has asked you to estimate the costs and benefits of the current law and the proposed new law.

What kind of evaluation is called for here? What evaluative questions and issues would you address?

2. Exhibit 1-J in the Rossi-Freeman text summarizes a monitoring evaluation of a school lunch program, and Exhibit 1-K summarizes an impact evaluation of an infant day care program. Review these exhibits and the discussion of Campbell's and Cronbach's positions on pp. 29-32. Address the following questions:

(1). Which of these evaluations is more "scientific?"

(2). In your view, was it the case that the design and implementation of one evaluation had to be less scientific than the other?

(3). Can you suggest some ways of making each evaluation more scientific?

ADDITIONAL READING ASSIGNMENTS [Type or write clearly on separate sheets of paper.]

1. Examine newspapers and magazines for reports of the three types of evaluations discussed in Chapter 1. [Newspapers and magazines that regularly cover national politics are the best sources for this exercise. Among newspapers, the New York Times, the Washington Post, and the Christian Science Monitor provide the best coverage of major political events. Among magazines, Time, Newsweek, and U.S. News and World Report are good sources. Issues of these newspapers and magazines are available in most libraries.]

2. Locate examples of two evaluations in journals that report the results of evaluation research. Summarize each of them in a paragraph or two. [There are several journals and annual reviews that publish the results of evaluation research. See the bibliography in the Appendix for a list of journals publishing evaluation studies. Your professor can also provide you with a list of journals in the fields relevant to your interests.]

CHAPTER 2

Diagnostic Procedures

REVIEW OF THE CHAPTER

•Social problems are objective phenomena, but they are also social constructions that emerge from the interests and values of the society and the stakeholders involved. Nevertheless, in the case of efforts to deal with most social problems, knowledge is required about the problem and the fates of past efforts to intervene. Reliable and valid research information about social problems is necessary as the basis for the devising of interventions. [See pp. 60-64.]

•A variety of procedures are used for identifying and defining social problems. Available social indicators can provide useful historical trends. Surveys of informed, "key persons," studies of agency records, and community surveys and censuses are common ways of approaching social problem identification. [See pp. 64-81.]

•Specifying the target population involves:

...a clear definition of target units.

...deciding whether targets are to be reached directly or indirectly.

...estimating the size (number) and distribution of targets.

...establishing rules of inclusion and exclusion as part of target definition.

...understanding needs from several perspectives. [See pp. 85-102.]

•Program planners should select a target population in a way that maximizes sensitivity and specificity. Efforts should be made to avoid overinclusion and underinclusion. [See pp. 98-99.]

•Among the important concepts used in selecting program targets are:

...incidence and prevalence.

...population at risk.

...sensitivity and specificity.

...need and demand.

...rates. [See pp. 96-101.]

REVIEW QUESTIONS

1. Give an example of what can happen when diagnostic information is not carefully collected.

2. Briefly define direct target and indirect target.

   (1). direct target

   (2). indirect target

3. Define "target boundary."

4. Briefly explain the distinction between incidence and prevalence.

5. Discuss briefly the importance of estimating sensitivity and specificity in identifying the targets of a program.

6. Briefly explain the distinction between need and demand.

7. What are two reasons some programs have a fairly loose definition of the target population?

   (1).

   (2).

8. List one strength and one weakness of the key person approach.

   (1). strength

   (2). weakness

9. List two considerations in judging the usefulness of an "indicator."

    (1).

    (2).

10. What is the major difference between a census and a survey?

SHORT EXERCISES

1. Discuss the different surveys for target estimation used in Exhibits 2-G and 2-J and evaluate the usefulness of each one.

2. Briefly distinguish between direct and indirect target populations.

3. Discuss the definition of poverty in Exhibit 2-K in terms of:

    (1). boundaries

    (2). varying perspectives on target specification

    (3). sensitivity

    (4). specificity

4. Using your community as an example, explain the difference between collecting information on the incidence of poverty and on the prevalence of poverty.

5. Discuss the use of the key person and survey techniques for estimating the prevalence of poverty in your community. Are there reasons to believe that these two techniques would produce different estimates of the prevalence of poverty? In which of these estimates would you have more confidence, and why?

DESIGN AND ANALYSIS TASKS [Write or type on separate sheets of paper.]

1. Three hypothetical programs are described below. The descriptions include the number of full-time and part-time staff. Using this information, choose the most appropriate technique or techniques for identifying and/or estimating the size of the target population. Explain why you think each technique is appropriate.

   (a) Teenage Drug Abuse Program: The school system in a large southern city has experienced increased problems with drug and alcohol abuse in the middle, junior, and high schools in the system. The State Department of Education has begun a program which provides money to school systems that implement programs to minimize drug abuse.

   In order to receive funds, the school system must provide reliable and documented estimates of the number of students in its system who might benefit from the program. More specifically, the Department of Education requires information on both the population in need (actual drug abusers) and the population at risk (potential drug abusers).

   The administrative offices of the school system include the following staff: one superintendent, three assistant superintendents, three secretaries, and one bookkeeper. What would be the most economical way for the school system to estimate the population at risk and the population in need? Once the program begins, what would be the most economical way to identify current drug abusers and students who are especially prone to abuse drugs?

   (b) Special Education for Children with Learning Disabilities: In many southern states, small rural schools with two to three teachers and 20 to 50 students fall under the jurisdiction of a county superintendent. In one of these counties, there are 20 such schools. The total number of students is 976. These students are in grades one to eight.

   The State's Department of Education is beginning a program to provide special materials and training to rural schools that have at least three children with some kind of learning disability. The office of the County Superintendent consists of the superintendent and his secretary.

   What would be the most economical and efficient way for the County Superintendent to determine which of his 20 schools qualified for this assistance? Once the program begins, what would be the most economical and efficient way to distinguish the eligible participants from those who are not eligible to participate?

   (c) Housing for the Homeless: The Salvation Army in a small midwestern city (65,000) is interested in providing shelter for families who have lost their housing either through eviction or some other "forced" move. In order to request federal emergency housing assistance funds to support the program, the Army must provide an estimate of the number of families that might participate in the program.

The Salvation Army staff consists of a captain and a secretary-administrative assistant. Two volunteers work an average of ten hours per week. What would be the best way for the Army to estimate the size of the target population? What would be the best way for the Army to identify eligible participants after the program begins?

2. The Urban League in a large eastern city is concerned about the level of alcohol abuse in one neighborhood in the city. Although concerned with alcohol abuse in the total population, they especially want information on alcohol abuse among Blacks.

There are 1200 persons over 18 living in the target neighborhood. In order to estimate rates of alcohol abuse, the Urban League collected information from a random sample of 50 adults in this neighborhood.

The indicator of alcohol abuse that was used was a questionnaire item, as follows: "Do you drink enough to become intoxicated at least once each week?" Information on race, sex, and age was also collected.

This information was coded as follows:

Variable Name	Columns	Values
I.D. Number	1-2	1-50
Race	3	1=white; 2=Black; 3=other
Sex	4	1=Male; 2=Female
Age	5-6	Years of age, from 18-99
Alcohol Abuse	7	1=yes; 2=no

Below, the information collected from respondents is listed by case. The left-hand number is the data for column one, the second number from the left for column 2, and so on. Using the data collected from these respondents, compile a table which gives the rates of alcohol abuse by age, race, and sex.

If you have access to a computer, use the data for all 50 cases. If you are doing the exercise without a computer, use the first ten cases. Analyze the data so that you can answer the following questions:

1) How many blacks would you estimate live in this neighborhood?

2) What racial group seems to have the highest prevalence of alcohol abuse?

3) Are males more prone to alcohol abuse than females?

4) Which combination of race, sex, and age has the highest prevalence of alcohol abuse?

5) Estimate the number of people in the neighborhood who abuse alcohol.

6) Estimate the number of blacks in the neighborhood who abuse alcohol.

Data

```
0111670  0222990  0311181  0432400  0521260
0632241  0721371  0821370  0931190  1022211
1121461  1221470  1331490  1431490  1512181
1612181  1721431  1822260  1921531  2011490
2122351  2232360  2331631  2421181  2522411
2621420  2721430  2821441  2921311  3022311
3132330  3231340  3321350  3421361  3521371
3622381  3722390  3821511  3921520  4021531
4121450  4222550  4322560  4422350  4531751
4621251  4721241  4821350  4932180  5022630
```

3. Exhibit 2-P provides crime victimization rates for the United States in 1986. Use those rates to answer the following:

a) If your community had 2000 white women between 25 and 34, how many women would have been victimized in that year?

b) If you were interested in providing counseling to adolescent victims (under 20) what does the information tell you about the race and gender of the staff that you would plan to hire?

c) In addition to the information on the age, ethnicity and gender of the victims, what two or three other characteristics might you want to know about in defining the population for a program of counseling them?

ADDITIONAL READING ASSIGNMENTS [Use separate sheets of paper.]

1. Review recent issues of newspapers and magazines for a story on defining the target population of a program. In particular, you might look for a controversy over broadening or narrowing the boundaries of a target population. Briefly summarize the major issues in the language of Chapter 2.

2. Read "Estimating statewide health-risk behavior: a comparison of telephone and key informant survey approaches" by E. Deaux and J.W. Callaghan. The complete reference for this article is given in Exhibit 2-E on p. 73. List their major conclusions. Do you find their argument convincing? Why or why not? Outline the use of another technique for estimating the prevalence of health-risk behavior in this setting. Discuss the strengths and weaknesses of your approach relative to the key informant and telephone survey approaches.

CHAPTER 3

Tailoring Evaluations

REVIEW OF THE CHAPTER

- Evaluations of innovative programs will often involve:

  ...operationalizing objectives for the program.

  ...developing the intervention model.

  ...defining the target population.

  ...designing the delivery system. [See pp. 111-135 in the text.]

- There are important differences between general goals and specific objectives. [See pp. 112-117 in the text.]

- Developing an intervention or impact model is an important part of program planning. An impact model includes:

  ...a causal hypothesis.

  ...an intervention hypothesis.

  ...an action hypothesis. [See pp. 119-123 in the text.]

- Even well-conceived interventions cannot be effective without a carefully developed delivery system. [See pp. 133-135 in the text.]

- Most evaluation efforts in this country involve the assessment of established programs [See pp. 142-144 in the text.]

- The evaluation of established programs often involves a pre-evaluation or evaluability assessment. The steps in such an assessment include:

  ...preparing a program description.

  ...interviewing program personnel.

  ...scouting the program.

...developing an evaluable program model.

...identifying evaluation users.

...achieving agreement to proceed. [See pp. 145-151 in the text.]

• One frequent type of evaluation of an established program is an accountability study. The most common types of data collected in these studies provide accountability information on:

...program impact.

...program efficiency.

...coverage.

...service delivery activities.

...finances

...conformity with legal requirements. [See pp. 151-153 in the text.]

• Fine-tuning existing programs involves five basic tasks:

...reappraising objectives and outcomes.

...identifying possible program modifications.

...assessing reputability.

...replanning and redesigning a program.

...planning and implementing evaluation to monitor changes and assess impact of fine-tuning. [See pp. 154-158.]

REVIEW QUESTIONS

1. Briefly outline the distinction often made by evaluators between goals and objectives.

2. List the four rules for specifying objectives discussed by Shortell and Richardson in Exhibit 3-C.

   (1).

   (2).

   (3).

   (4).

3. Briefly define:

   (1). causal hypothesis

   (2). intervention hypothesis

   (3). action hypothesis

4. List three sources of impact model hypotheses.

   (1).

   (2).

   (3).

5. Briefly discuss the meaning of manipulability and feasibility of impact models.

   (1). manipulability

   (2). feasibility

6. List three of the elements of delivery systems that are often monitored.

   (1).

   (2).

   (3).

7. Briefly outline the major similarities and differences between formative studies and program simulations.

8. List the conditions that make an evaluability assessment a worthwhile undertaking.

9. Briefly outline the differences between continuous and cross-sectional evaluations.

10. List the three distinctions in style between evaluations of innovative programs and evaluations of established programs.

(1).

(2).

(3).

SHORT EXERCISES

1. Select a major social program (such as Social Security, Medicaid, or Headstart) and list one of its goals and one of its objectives.

(1). goal

(2). objective

2. Using the rules for specifying objectives in Exhibit 3-C, list one goal and specify one associated objective of this course.

    (1). goal

    (2). objective

3. One impact model that underlies the Social Security system in this country might be summarized as follows:

    Inadequate savings lead to an increased likelihood of poverty after leaving the labor force. Therefore a compulsory savings plan is proposed so that individuals have adequate savings after leaving the labor force. Identify the:

    (1). causal hypothesis

    (2). intervention hypothesis

4. Using your personal experience, briefly outline a workable delivery system for financial aid to college students at your college or university.

DESIGN AND ANALYSIS TASKS [Answer on separate sheets of paper.]

1. The following is a description of a hypothetical program:

> The staff of the Women's Resource Center in Smallville has become increasingly concerned about the high levels of unemployment and underemployment and the low earnings of female heads of households. According to the information that is available from other social service organizations in the city, these problems result in many becoming unable to make rent payments, to pay utility bills and to provide needed clothing for their school-age children.

> Existing public and private programs are ineffective in solving this problem. Because of the critical nature of the problem, the Women's Resource Center decided to explore ways to deal with the economic situation faced by these families.

> Two searches for relevant information were undertaken. One group examined the literature on the determinants of socioeconomic status to identify causal factors of low economic status. A second group examined sources of program support for initiatives to assist disadvantaged individuals, including families with female heads of households.

> The first group discovered that the literature on economic status indicated that education, skills, and experience were among the most important determinants of success in the labor force. This group also discovered that jobs and persons were sometimes not matched because individuals did not engage in effective job search strategies. They reasoned that if single heads of households had more effective ways of searching for jobs, they would have lower levels of unemployment and underemployment. Improved job searching opportunities were regarded as an easier and less costly variable to change than education, training, or experience.

> The second group discovered that there was money available from a local private foundation which would support limited, small-scale programs designed to have an impact on well-defined populations. They were advised to submit a two-page concept paper that outlined the intervention model of their proposed program and the way the program would be delivered. Provide a "first draft" of this paper.

2. The following is a description of a second hypothetical program to deal with the same problem by the Women's Resource Center in Uptag City:

The staff of the Uptag City Center became aware of a state agency which funded peer counseling programs. The idea behind these counseling programs is that persons from the target population can provide better counselling services to their peers than professionally trained counsellors. In this case, heads of female households would be counseling other heads of such households. It is believed that such efforts can lead to improved morale and an increase in the ability of the persons counseled to deal with the social and psychological consequences of unemployment.

Two of the three intervention model hypotheses are missing from this program description. Which two are they? What problems would one face in evaluating this program?

3. Using the program descriptions outlined in Exercises 1 and 2 above, discuss whether the following questions can be answered about each of the described programs:

   (1). To what extent are the hypotheses in each program related to their causal hypotheses?

   (2). To what extent are their causal hypotheses related to their outcome hypotheses?

   (3). To what extent are the intervention variables related to their outcome hypotheses?

4. If you could interview the manager of a teen-age recreation program designed to reduce juvenile delinquency for, say, 15 minutes, what questions would you ask to gain information on the following (remember, the manager has not had this course):

   (1). The intervention model of the program.

   (2). The rationale underlying the program.

   (3). Alternative programs that might be more effective.

   (4). The objectives and how they are measured.

ADDITIONAL READING ASSIGNMENTS [Use separate sheets of paper.]

1. Review the discussion in Exhibit 3-A of the history of the New Jersey-Pennsylvania Negative Income Tax Experiment (pp. 108-109). If possible, briefly review the section of the monograph from which this excerpt was taken. (See reference in Exhibit 3-A.) Using this information, outline the impact models of "traditional" welfare programs and the negative income tax experiment.

2. Locate a journal article that reports the results of an evaluation or that provides a description of a social service delivery program. (See Appendix for journals that publish evaluation reports.)   Based on this article:

   (1). Identify the intervention, causal, and outcome hypotheses.

   (2). Outline and discuss any ambiguities and/or inconsistencies in the intervention model.

   (3). To the extent possible given the content of the article and your knowledge of the literature, evaluate the extent to which the program is based on a careful analysis of literature on the measurement of the outcome variable.

CHAPTER 4

Program Monitoring for Evaluation and Management

REVIEW OF THE CHAPTER

•Program monitoring is an important activity at all stages of development and implementation. [See pp. 164-174.]

•The types of program accountability include:

...coverage accountability.

...service delivery accountability.

...fiscal accountability.

...legal accountability.

•Determining the actual participation of program targets is an important part of program monitoring. Among the issues involved in assessing participation are:

...coverage and bias.

...the quality of program records.

...deciding when surveys of participants and/or the community are desirable and feasible.

...identifying the characteristics of utilizers, eligibles, and dropouts. [See pp. 175-187.]

•Errors in delivering services include:

...incomplete or no treatment.

...wrong treatment.

...unstandardized treatment. [See pp. 188-191.]

• The important components of a delivery system include:

...access (the structural and organizational arrangements that provide opportunities for and operate to facilitate program participation).

...services defined in terms of time, costs, procedures, or products. [See pp. 188-197.]

• Among the sources of data for monitoring evaluations are:

...observational data.

...service record data.

...data from program staff.

...data from program participants. [See pp. 197-209.]

• The analysis of monitoring data usually addresses:

...a basic description of the program.

...the differences in program implementation at different sites.

...the extent to which the implemented program resembles the designed program. [See pp. 209-211.]

REVIEW QUESTIONS

1. Briefly describe the relationship between program monitoring and outcome evaluation.

2. Briefly define:

      (1). coverage

      (2). bias

3. Briefly outline:

      (1). one way of measuring undercoverage

      (2). two ways of measuring overcoverage

      (3). the formula for measuring the efficiency of coverage

4. List three ways of promoting the reliability of program records.

    (1).

    (2).

    (3).

5. List three evaluation questions that arise in monitoring access to services.

    (1).

    (2).

    (3).

6. Briefly explain why program monitoring is most successful when programs are kept as simple as possible.

7. List three typical ways of making systematic observations.

        (1).

        (2).

        (3).

8. List three guidelines for using service record data in implementation evaluations.

        (1).

        (2).

        (3).

SHORT EXERCISES

1. Discuss the relationship between "creaming," coverage, and bias.

2. Discuss the meaning of the following values of "coverage efficiency" computed using the formula on p. 179. What are possible responses by program administrators to these values?

   (1). -60

   (2). +50

   (3). +95

3. List two ways of improving the coverage of the Food Stamp Program discussed in Exhibit 4-D on pp. 182-183.

   (1).

   (2).

4. Compare the relative strengths and weaknesses of using service provider data and program participant data in evaluating program implementation.

5. Outline an MIS (Management Information System) for the Food Stamp Program of Exhibit 4-D.

DESIGN AND ANALYSIS TASKS [Type or write your answers on separate sheets of paper.]

The design and analysis tasks that follow are based on a fictitious program described below:

Assume that you have been hired by a university to evaluate the implementation of the Assistance Program offered by the University Study Skills Laboratory.

The first responsibility of this laboratory is to locate students whose study skills need to be improved in order for them to be successful in college. At present the laboratory relies on the identification of problems by the students themselves or referrals by instructors, who may suggest to students that they take advantage of the study skills laboratory. Any student who feels he or she might benefit from participating in any part of the program is allowed to participate, regardless of how well or how poorly the student may be doing in his/her work.

The second responsibility of the laboratory is to provide training in the form of a three-credit course in study skills. Three sections of this course are offered each semester. In this course, students learn how to use the library, read textbooks critically, take notes, and engage in other activities that may lead to increased success in their academic work.

Third, counselors at the laboratory work with students on an individual level. Each student is asked to visit with a counselor once each week for approximately one hour. During these sessions, the student and counselor discuss the ways in which general study skills may be applied to specific courses with which the students may be having problems. Students may enroll in the study skills course and be individually counseled or utilize either part of the program separately.

The Study Skills Laboratory is part of University Student Services. The staff consists of a director who also serves as a teacher. She teaches one section of the study skills course. There are two teacher-counselors who teach sections of the study skills course and also counsel students on an individual basis. The fourth staff member is a full-time counselor who does not have any course teaching responsibilities.

The provost of the university has become concerned about programs such as the Study Skills Laboratory which are not part of the traditional academic operation of the university and which consume a large amount of resources. He has requested the following information from the director of the program.

First, the provost is interested in what kinds of students are utilizing the program. Further, of those students who really need the program, what percentage is actually using it? How many students who do not need the program are utilizing it? Do the students using the program differ in measurable ways from all students and students in need who do not use the program? What is the drop-out rate from the program, and who is dropping out?

Second, the provost is interested in what services are being delivered and the way in which they are being delivered. How much time is spent with each student? How is the time of the director, teacher-counselors, and counselor spent? What is the cost per student served of the program? What techniques are used to teach students? What is being taught?

In your initial discussion with the program staff and the provost, you have discovered that some information is already available: First, the program maintains some basic information on participants in the program. This information includes SAT scores, grades, counseling record, participation in the study skills course, race, size of the high school, major, age, and sex. Second, all of this information, with the exception of counseling record and participation in the study skills course, is also available for students who have not participated in the program. Third, there are brief reports on each counseling session held by each counselor. In addition, you have been given permission to interview staff members and students and to sit in on the study skills class and any counseling session.

1. Identify those questions that deal with target participation. Do they deal with coverage, bias, utilizers, eligibles, and/or dropouts?

2. Which questions have to do with service delivery issues?

3. Assume that you have decided on using 2.0 on a 4.0 GPA scale as the cutoff for identifying the population in need. How would you answer the coverage and bias questions raised by the provost? How would you estimate the number and characteristics of utilizers, eligibles, and dropouts?

4. Specify the program "elements" (time, cost, procedures, products). Outline a monitoring strategy.

5. Outline a report that you would present to the provost in which you reported your results.

40

ADDITIONAL READING ASSIGNMENTS [Use separate sheets of paper.]

1. Read "Program implementation versus program design" by David B. Robertson. The complete reference for this article is given in Exhibit 4-C. Outline the major differences between the design of the USES and the implementation of the USES. Discuss the difficulties these differences cause for evaluators who are interested in determining the impact of the USES.

CHAPTER 5

Strategies for Impact Assessment

REVIEW OF THE CHAPTER

• The prerequisites of assessing the impact of an intervention are:

...well articulated objectives.

...sound implementation. [See p. 218.]

• The critical issue in impact evaluation is whether or not a program produces more of an effect than would have occurred either without the intervention or with an alternative intervention. [See pp. 218-221.]

• The "good enough" rule in choosing evaluation designs means that the evaluator should choose the best possible design, taking into account practicality and feasibility. [See pp. 220-221.]

• Gross outcomes include all changes in an outcome measure that occur during and subsequent to program participation; net outcomes are those impacts that can be attributed to the intervention. [See pp. 221-222.]

• Some of the most important possible confounding factors include:

...endogenous change.

...secular drift.

...interfering events.

...maturational trends.

...uncontrolled selection. [See pp. 222-225.]

• Some of the most important design effects that threaten the validity of impact assessments are:

...stochastic effects.

...measurement unreliability.

...lack of validity in measurement.

... "Hawthorne Effect."

...delivery system contaminants.

...missing values.

...sample design effects. [See pp. 226-240.]

• "Controls" are the method by which what would have happened, absent the treatment, is estimated. Approaches for establishing controls include:

...randomized controls.

...regression-discontinuity controls.

...matched constructed controls.

...statistically equated controls.

...reflexive controls.

...generic controls. [See pp. 240-241.]

• A meta-evaluation involves a review of the existing evidence on the effectiveness of a social program from previous evaluations. [See p. 253.]

• Producing relatively precise estimates of net effects requires data that are quantifiable and systematically and uniformly collected. [See p. 254.]

• To provide the basis for valid statements about whether or not a program results in significant effects, an impact evaluation must be reproducible and generalizable. [See pp. 255-257.]

REVIEW QUESTIONS

1. List three obstacles to the conduct of impact assessments.

(1).

(2).

(3).

2. What are the three contributing factors to the gross outcomes of a program?

      (1).

      (2).

      (3).

3. Define and give an example of "selection bias."

4. Define and give examples of Type I and Type II errors.

      (1). Type I error

      (2). Type II error

5. Why is it difficult to eradicate unreliability completely?

6. Briefly explain the relationship between reliability and validity.

7. What are the two important characteristics of a good outcome measure?

(1).

(2).

8. Briefly define the term "Hawthorne Effect."

9. Discuss the three major tasks and three major errors in drawing a sample.

(1).

(2).

(3).

10. Briefly explain the major differences between "true" experiments, "constructed controls" studies, and "statistical controls" studies.

SHORT EXERCISES

1. Using student performance on a test as the outcome measure and classroom lectures as the "treatment," discuss the difference between gross and net outcomes.

2. Why is uncontrolled selection a problem in assessing the net effect of graduate school on life-time earnings?

3. Briefly explain the difference between endogenous change and maturational trends. Give an example of each.

4. Explain why the issue of validity is more difficult to deal with than the issue of reliability.

5. Give an example of a "proxy" outcome measure.

6. Explain the importance of coverage issues in choosing a design for an impact evaluation.

DESIGN AND ANALYSIS TASKS [Type or write your answers on separate sheets of paper.]

It is possible to think of the classroom as a social program with student learning as the outcome of interest. More specifically, concentrate on the class in which you are using this workbook, and consider the issues involved in evaluating the impact of the class.

1. What are some of the obstacles to evaluating the impact of the class on students?

2. What are some possible extraneous confounding factors that might affect what students have learned by the end of the semester?

3. What are some possible outcome measures that you could use to investigate the impact of the class?

   a. How would you assess the reliability of these measures?

   b. How would you assess the validity of these measures?

4. Which of the designs discussed on p. 242 could you use to assess the impact of the class? Which of the designs could you not use to assess the impact of the class?

5. Do you believe that qualitative or quantitative data would be most useful in assessing the impact of the class?

6. Assuming that you could use the best possible design of those that are feasible, assess the generalizability and reproducibility of the results.

ADDITIONAL READING ASSIGNMENTS [Use separate sheets of paper.]

1. Read the first several chapters in either Guba and Lincoln (1981) or Patton (1980). [Full references are listed in Rossi and Freeman.]:

   a. Briefly outline their argument in favor of using qualitative approaches to evaluations.

   b. Compare their position to that of Rossi and Freeman in the textbook. Which view do you agree with the most? Why?

2. Review the position of Campbell and Stanley (1966) on the trade-off between reproducibility and generalizability:

   a. Briefly outline their position.

   b. Compare their position to that of Rossi and Freeman in the textbook.

   c. Which view do you think is most correct? Why?

CHAPTER 6

Randomized Designs for Impact Assessment

REVIEW OF THE CHAPTER

• The choice of units of analysis in an impact assessment is determined by the nature of the intervention involved. [See pp. 261-262.]

• Those participating in the program are designated as the experimental group and those to whom they are compared are designated as the control group [See pp. 263-264.]

• Randomization is the surest way to obtain comparability between experimental and control groups. [See pp. 264-268.]

• Surrogates for randomized selection include

...systematic assignment from serialized lists.

..."natural" randomization in unplanned interventions. [See pp. 273-277.]

• Analyses of randomized experiments range from simple, straightforward comparisons of percentages and means to highly complex multiple regression and time-series analyses. Both the complexity of the design and the analytical sophistication of the evaluators are determinants of the design strategy. [See pp. 278-290.]

• Limitations on the use of randomized experiments in assessing the impact of social programs include:

...randomized experiments are not fruitful in the very early stages of program development.

...some persons have ethical qualms about randomization.

...the treatment delivered in an actual program may vary considerably from that delivered in a controlled experimental setting.

...randomized experiments are costly and time-consuming.

...randomized experiments are unlikely to have high generalizability or external validity. [See pp. 190-293.]

REVIEW QUESTIONS

1. Explain why randomized experiments and quasi-experimental designs can only be used to assess the impacts of partial coverage programs.

2. Write out and explain the formula for computing the net effects of a program with data from experimental and control groups.

3. List the three prerequisites for comparability between experimental and control groups.

    (1).

    (2).

    (3).

4. Briefly explain the difference between randomization and random sampling.

5. Define the meaning of the phrase "stochastically generated difference between experimental and control groups."

6. Briefly explain the relationship between randomization and unbiased selection.

7. What must we know about a serialized list of targets before using it to assign units to experimental and control groups?

8. Give two reasons for taking many measures before, during, and after an intervention.

   (1).

   (2).

9. Why are random experiments especially appropriate for testing new pilot programs?

10. List the circumstances under which large-scale randomized field experiments are most appropriate.

SHORT EXERCISES

1. Describe or make up a full-coverage social program and a partial coverage program. Would it be possible to use a randomized experiment to evaluate the full coverage program? Why or why not?

2. Can we be confident that Plaza Sesamo had the effects that are reported in Exhibit 6-A? Is it possible to rule out the possibility of maturational change? Is there some feature of the design of the experiment that allows us to rule out this explanation in this particular situation? Is it possible to rule out a "Hawthorne Effect"?

3. Is it possible to generalize the results of Plaza Sesamo to other groups in other settings? For example, what are some of the dangers involved in generalizing to children who are not in daycare centers? What are some of the dangers involved in generalizing to children in other countries?

4. Are there any ethical considerations in this experiment? Was it ethical to prevent children in the control group from viewing Plaza Sesamo?

5. Is it possible to generalize the results of the randomized control experiment summarized in Exhibit 6-B to other groups in other settings? First, is it possible to generalize these results to other children with chronic illnesses in other places in the United States? What are some factors which one would have to take into account in making such generalizations? Second, is it possible to conclude that home care is an effective strategy in any situation? Why or why not?

DESIGN AND ANALYSIS TASKS [Type or write your answers on separate sheets of paper.]

1. Exhibit 6-D in the textbook describes and provides the results from the Baltimore LIFE Experiment. Although the major findings and conclusions are provided in the exhibit, it is worthwhile to think more carefully about these results in the context of some of the issues raised in Chapters 5 and 6.

    a. Use the results in Table 6-D.1 to illustrate the difference between gross outcomes and net outcomes.

    b. Suppose that when you report the results in Table 6-D.1 to agency personnel, someone argues that providing money to individuals seems to increase the likelihood of being arrested for a serious personal crime (murder, rape, assault, etc.). Assume that this individual has had no training in statistics or methods. How would you explain to him or her that the -8.4% difference indicates a "real" effect, but the +3.2% difference does not? (Hint: Simply stating that the latter difference is not statistically significant will not suffice in this situation.)

    c. Table 6-D.2 contains the results of a regression analysis with the dependent variable equal to 1 if the individual is arrested on a property related charge and 0 otherwise. The effect for membership in the experimental group is -.083 with a standard error of .041. Compare the meaning of this coefficient to the meaning of the -8.4% difference in Table 6-D.1. The effect for "Baltimore unemployment rate at time of release" in Table 6-D.2 is .041 with a standard error of .022. What does this mean? The effect of Race is .056 with a standard error of .064. What does this mean?

2. The Plaza Sesamo experiment reported on in Exhibit 6-A employed pretest-posttest control group design. This design has a number of strengths which are discussed in textbooks on experimental and evaluation research. (See, for example, Cook and Campbell, 1979, in the references in Rossi and Freeman.) There are, however, several alternatives to this design that could have been used to evaluate Plaza Sesamo. One of these is known as the posttest-only control group design. Another alternative is known as the Solomon Four-Group Design and is really a combination of the above two designs. There are others as well.

a. Select two alternatives to the Plaza Sesamo design (you may use one or both of the above as alternatives if you wish, or others you have learned about). Discuss the relative strengths and weaknesses of these designs compared with the one employed in the Plaza Sesamo study. Include a discussion not only of the scientific merit of each design but a consideration of practical issues such as costs and ease of explaining the results to program administrators and others who may not have a background in experimental methods and research.

b. Use each of the alternative designs to construct a new Plaza Sesamo experiment. Discuss how you would select children for the experimental and control groups; when, how, and if pretests would be done; and when and how posttests would be done.

ADDITIONAL READING ASSIGNMENTS [Use separate sheets of paper.]

1. Read "Selecting a control group: an analysis of the randomization process in twelve social reform programs" by R. F. Conner in *Evaluation Quarterly* 1 (May): 195-244. Briefly summarize Conner's conclusions. Using the programs in this article as example, explain why there is no one best method of randomization.

2. Review the Fairweather and Tornatzky strategy of using small-scale randomized experiments in the development of halfway homes (the citation to Fairweather and Tornatzky, 1977, is included in the references in Rossi and Freeman). Why was this strategy more appropriate than a longitudinal field experiment in the area of their work?

CHAPTER 7

Quasi-Experimental Impact Assessments

REVIEW OF THE CHAPTER

•Quasi-experiments are designed used to estimate the impacts of partial coverage programs, when it is not feasible to undertake randomized experiments. [See pp. 298-299.]

•Ex ante quasi experiments are ones in which control groups are selected prior to program implementation and ex post are ones in which the controls are constructed after implementation. [See pp. 301-302.]

•The use of "constructed controls" involves identifying and selecting a group of potential targets comparable in essential respects to those exposed to treatment. The procedures used for selecting constructed control groups include:

...individual matching.

...aggregate matching.

...statistical control of selected differences. [See pp. 303-314.]

•Constructed and statistical controls are equivalent ways of proceeding, but some advantages lie in statistical controls. [See pp. 314-315.]

•Selection bias modelling is a sophisticated statistical procedure in which the evaluator tries to hold selection biases constant by modelling the processes that bring targets into a program [See pp. 318-319.]

•Regression-discontinuity designs are appropriate when participants are chosen according to some fixed procedure. [See pp. 319-320.]

•The use of generic controls in assessing impact is rare since we seldom have firm knowledge about what ordinarily happens in the course of social action. [See pp. 320-322.]

•Cross-sectional approaches to impact assessment have some advantages, but also some important limitations. [See pp. 326-329.]

REVIEW QUESTIONS

1. What are the important differences between assessing the impact of a program with a quasi-experiment relative to assessing the impact with a true experiment?

2. Give an example of a program for which a regression-discontinuity design is appropriate (not using the ones in the book).

3. Briefly explain the difference between individual and aggregate matching.

4. What are the four characteristics that are useful in devising constructed controls?

   (1).

   (2).

   (3).

   (4).

5. Under what circumstances should generic controls be used?

6. What are retrospective measures? When should they be used?

7. Briefly describe the limitations of using statistical controls with cross-sectional data for impact evaluations.

SHORT EXERCISES

(Note: Questions 1 to 3 refer to Exhibit 7-C.)

1. Can we be confident in the results? One of the problems that is of concern in quasi-experimental research is what the text terms "uncontrolled selection." Is uncontrolled selection a potential problem in this evaluation? Does the use of statistical controls as discussed in this exhibit help resolve this problem?

2. Can the results of the evaluation be generalized to other groups in other settings? Some argue that an advantage of quasi-experimental research is that it avoids the artificiality of experiments and thus leads to results that are more generalizable. Are the results of this evaluation more generalizable than the results from a hypothetical experiment in which students were randomly assigned to experimental and control groups? Why or why not?

3. Does the design of this evaluation raise any ethical issues? Some argue that another advantage of quasi-experimental research is that it avoids some of the ethical issues raised by the random assignment of individuals to potentially beneficial treatments and others to no treatment. Does the design of this evaluation represent an "ethical" improvement over an experimental design? Why or why not?

Design and Analysis Tasks

1. Design an evaluation--using nonequivalent control groups--to assess the impact of providing high school students with home personal computers and software that provides reviews of the subjects they are studying in school. Make certain you include:

    a. How you would select the control group.

    b. When you would observe the experimental and control groups.

    c. What are some alternative forms of information you could collect from the experimental and control groups?

    d. What are some statistical tests that might be appropriate?

2. Design an evaluation of the impact of being in a foster home on income achievement in adulthood using a cross sectional survey of adults aged 25-40.

    a. How would you compare adults with foster home experience with those who did not have that experience?

    b. What information would you collect from the adults to use as statistical controls?

    c. How confident would you feel in the findings? What are their limitations?

3. Read "The first year of the education voucher demonstration: A secondary analysis of student achievement test scores" by Wortman et al. The complete citation for this article is given in Rossi-Freeman in Exhibit 7-A. List the major conclusions of the authors regarding the impact of vouchers. Discuss why their conclusions were different from those of the initial external evaluation.

Chapter 8

Assessment of Full-Coverage Programs

REVIEW OF THE CHAPTER

• The evaluation of full coverage programs cannot be done by using control or comparison groups. Only reflexive controls and shadow controls can be used. [See pp. 334-335.]

• Non-uniform full-coverage programs can be evaluated for differential impact comparing variations in the program over jurisdictions. [See pp. 335-340.]

• The use of reflexive controls involves comparing participants in a program to themselves at a previous point or points in time. Alternative methods of using reflexive controls include:

      ...before-and-after studies.

      ...panel studies.

      ...time-series of aggregated data.

      ...time-series of individual data. [See pp. 340-351.]

• For programs in which it is difficult to compare persons with and without program experience or to examine changes over time, it may be necessary to use a form of shadow controls known as judgmental assessment. [See pp. 351-361.]

Review Questions

1. What are three problems with reflexive designs?

       (1).

       (2).

       (3).

9. What is the major advantage of panel studies over cross-sectional studies?

10. What sources of data should be considered by experts in evaluating the impact of a program?

Short Exercises

1. Can we be confident in the results of the evaluation described in Exhibit 8-D (p. 344). Does the use of recalled TV exposure pose any problem? Must we be concerned about uncontrolled selection? What are some ways in which the children might have differed according to their viewing of TV?

2. Can the results of the evaluation discussed in Question 1 be generalized?

DESIGN AND ANALYSIS TASKS [Type or write your answers on separate sheets of paper.]

1. The exhibits in Chapter 8 provide illustrations of a number of full coverage evaluation designs. Select three of them and discuss the following: How would you convince action agency personnel that randomized and cross-sectional designs cannot be used for these programs?

2. In some states public welfare programs are administered by county agencies with each county having considerable discretion in defining eligibility. In one state with forty

counties, 15 counties will not give AFDC payments to husband-wife families, another 20 counties require that adults with no children under 6 must work 20 hours per week in public service jobs and the remaining counties do not have either provision. You have been asked to evaluate the impact of these variations on the length of time families remain on AFDC.

a. Design an evaluation for the state.

3. You have been asked by a local social agency that runs a program for terminally ill patients to help them select an evaluator who can assess the program's adequacy. What will you tell the agency to look for in getting an evaluator? How would you go about finding such a person?

ADDITIONAL READING ASSIGNMENTS [Use separate sheets of paper.]

1. Read "The effects of Massachusetts' Gun Control Law" by Deutsch and Alt. The complete citation for this article is given in Exhibit 7-K on p. 360. Are there any other designs appropriate to evaluate the Massachusetts' Gun Control Law? What are the limitations of the design and analysis provided?

CHAPTER 9

Measuring Efficiency

REVIEW OF THE CHAPTER

• Efficiency analyses provide a disciplined way of judging the worth of social programs. [See pp. 371-372.]

• How to do analyses of efficiency correctly is an issue of considerable controversy. [See pp. 371-376.]

• The major difference between cost-benefit and cost-effectiveness analyses is that the latter involves monetizing only program costs. [See pp. 371-376.]

• The first step in an efficiency analysis is to list the costs and benefits of the program. [See pp. 371-376.]

• Three accounting perspectives may be used for the analysis of social projects:

...individual participants or targets.

...program sponsors.

...communal aggregates. [See pp. 377-381.]

• The methods for monetizing program outcomes include:

...money measurements.

...market valuation.

...econometric estimation.

...hypothetical questions.

...observing political choices. [See pp. 381-387.]

• Sound efficiency analyses must consider:

...distributional considerations.

...externalities.

...discounting. [See pp. 388-393.]

REVIEW QUESTIONS

1. List three reasons why formal, complete efficiency analyses may be either impractical or
   unwise.

           (1).

           (2).

           (3).

2. Discuss the differences between ex ante and ex post efficiency analyses.

3. Why is there more controversy surrounding the conversion of program outcomes into
   monetary terms than the conversion of program inputs into monetary terms?

4. Define opportunity costs.

5. Which accounting perspective is likely to lead to higher benefit-to-cost ratios and why?

6. What are the two distinct problems raised by the specification, measurement, and valuation of costs and benefits?

        (1).

        (2).

7. Briefly explain the relevance of "shadow prices" in monetizing costs and benefits.

8. Briefly explain the difference between using weights and disaggregation in analyzing distributional considerations.

9. Why are the results of an analysis of efficiency sensitive to the choice of a discount rate?

10. Why should ex post cost-benefit analysis and cost-effectiveness analysis be viewed as components of a comprehensive evaluation?

SHORT EXERCISES

(Note: Exercises 1 to 4 refer to Exhibit 9-F.)

1. Define three potential benefits of the program from the standpoint of program administrators.

     (1).

     (2).

     (3).

2. Define three potential costs of the program from the standpoint of its clients.

3. Which of the ways of measuring costs and benefits would be most appropriate for measuring costs and benefits to participants in this situation? Why?

4. Should "discounting" be an important concern in this cost-benefit analysis? Why or why not?

(Note: Questions 5-7 refer to Exhibit 9-D.)

5. Was an effort made to ensure that the program had an effect before performing a cost-benefit analysis? Why is this an important task?

6. If one wished to do a cost-benefit analysis from the standpoint of program participants, what are some costs and benefits that could be examined?

7. Which of the ways of measuring costs and benefits discussed in the textbook were used in this evaluation?

(Note: Questions 8-9 refer to Exhibit 9-E.)

8. From whose standpoint are costs and benefits being defined?

9. Is discounting an important concern in this situation? Why or why not?

DESIGN AND ANALYSIS TASKS [Type or write your answers on separate sheets of paper.]

1. Refer to the LIFE experiment discussed in Chapter 6 in the textbook and used in the Chapter 6 exercises. In this exercise use the information which is available to you in Exhibit 6-D to design a cost-benefit analysis of this project:

    a. Which accounting perspective would you use to define costs and benefits? Why?

    b. Develop a list of costs and benefits from each of the three alternative accounting perspectives:

    (1). individual participants

    (2). program sponsors

    (3). communal aggregates

    c. Develop a list of measures of costs and benefits from your chosen accounting perspective using one of the following techniques. If you feel that one or more of these techniques is not appropriate in this situation, please explain why.

    (1). money measurements

    (2). market valuation

    (3). econometric estimation

    (4). hypothetical questions

    (5). observing political choices

    d. Discuss whether or not discounting will be an issue in your cost-benefit analysis.

2. Design a cost-effectiveness analysis of Plaza Sesamo, which is discussed in Exhibit 6-A.

    a. Assume that you are asked to be involved at the beginning of the experiment. Will this be an ex ante or an ex post analysis?

    b. Would a cost-benefit analysis also be appropriate?

    c. Develop a list of costs and benefits from each of the three alternative accounting perspectives of:

(1). students

(2). schools

(3). the country of Mexico

d. Choose a perspective. Why do you think this perspective is most appropriate in this situation?

e. What are some distributional considerations that would be important in this situation? What are some possible externalities?

ADDITIONAL READING ASSIGNMENTS [Use separate sheets of paper.]

1. Read "Cost-effectiveness analysis in evaluation research" by H. M Levin. The complete citation for this article appears on p. 466 of the text. Outline the steps one must go through to do a cost-effectiveness analysis.

2. Read "The economic returns to increased educational spending" by Ribich and Murphy. The complete citation for this article appears on p. 469 of the text. Outline their approach to dealing with distributional considerations.

CHAPTER 10

The Social Context of Evaluation

REVIEW OF THE CHAPTER

- Differences between applied and basic social research include:

    ...a focus on "good enough" methods vs. "best" methods.

    ...interdisciplinary and multi-method research vs. specialization.

    ...practical vs. intellectual concerns.

    ...the audience to whom the report of results is addressed. [See pp. 405-406.]

- The rationale for doing applied work is to influence the actions and thinking of the broad category of persons who effect social change. [See pp. 406-420.]

- Evaluation is best described as a "near group" rather than as a profession. [See pp. 430-443.]

- Three ways of utilizing evaluations are:

    ...direct or instrumental use.

    ...conceptual use.

    ...persuasive use. [See pp. 443-452.]

REVIEW QUESTIONS

1. Briefly outline the intellectual roots of evaluation research.

2. Briefly outline the two routes to training and education for being an evaluator.

(1).

(2).

3. Briefly consider the consequences of educational diversity in training evaluators.

4. Discuss the relative strengths and weaknesses of inside and outside evaluations.

5. What are the two major consequences of having multiple stakeholders in most evaluations?

    (1).

    (2).

6. Identify some of the major strains that occur because of multiple stakeholders.

7. Define political time and evaluation time.

8. Discuss the differences between policy significance and statistical significance.

9. What are the five conditions that typically affect utilization?

      (1).

      (2).

      (3).

      (4).

      (5).

10. Briefly outline the guidelines suggested by Solomon and Shortell for maximizing the utilization of evaluation research.

11. List three reasons for expecting continued support of evaluation activities.

(1).

(2).

(3).

SHORT EXERCISES

1. If you were asked during a presentation of a finding on educational evaluation to a school board, "What do you mean by statistical significance?" how would you answer?

2. If you were asked to add topics to the Rossi-Freeman volume, what would they be?

3. If you were asked what topics to delete from the Rossi-Freeman text, what would they be? Defend your answer.

4. If a graduate student came to you and asked whether she would be better off being trained as an evaluator in one of the social science departments or one of the professional schools at her university, what would you advise her? Defend your answer.

5. If the executives of a major company asked you to lecture for an hour about evaluating the social programs that their company donates money to each year, what would the outline of your lecture look like?

DESIGN AND ANALYSIS TASKS [Type or write on separate sheets of paper.]

1. Select a journal article that evaluates a social program that was published in 1988 or later. [See Appendix for relevant professional journals.] Provide a critique of it from a methodological standpoint. What information would be necessary to make it more likely that the findings will be utilized?

2. Take the information in the article you selected above and write a one page "press release" on it. If the director of a major planning organization asked you to review the article and advise him if he should take it seriously and wanted you to do so in less than 1000 words, what would the first draft of your paper look like?

3. If you had to write the job description for the "perfect" evaluator who was going to be recruited to direct a $10 million national evaluation of the impacts and benefits to costs of building a "new city" for two million persons, what would it look like?

4. Instead of the "new city evaluation" described in 3., suppose it was an evaluation of extending high school to five years rather than four.

5. If you had to advise a large evaluation team about doing an evaluation of a major medical care program, what would you advise them in terms of relating to policy makers and stakeholders? Suppose they were to hire you to deal with these groups for a three-year period. How would you go about your work?

ADDITIONAL READING ASSIGNMENTS [Answer on separate sheets of paper.]

1. Read "Furthering the applied side of sociology" by Freeman and Rossi. The complete citation for this article appears on p. 462 in the text. Outline their views on how to encourage applied research in sociology. Can their major conclusions be generalized to other disciplines?

2. Read "Management of federally funded evaluation teams" by Robert G. St. Pierre. This article is briefly summarized in Exhibit 10-G on p. 441 of Rossi-Freeman. Outline St. Pierre's views on how to assemble an efficient evaluation team.

APPENDIX

A Guide to the Evaluation Field and Its Literature

Prepared by

Peter H. Rossi
and
Richard A. Berk

"....'the complete policy researcher' must be a knowledgeable methodologist, a creative theoretician, a capable manager, and a skilled politician. This is not the job description for a graduate student who is never quite able to understand what internal validity is all about, whose conception of theory is limited to a terminological maze that makes no claims about how things 'work', and whose administrative skills are taxed by managing to get a dissertation typed and turned in on time." (from Herbert L. Costner, "Commentaries" in Demerath, Larsen and Schuessler (Eds.), Social Policy and Sociology (New York, Academic Press, 1975, p. 262).

Note: This annotated bibliography was first published as an Appendix to R. A. Berk and P. H. Rossi, *Thinking About Program Evaluation*, (Sage Publications 1990). It has been updated by Rossi and is published with the permission of R. A. Berk.

I: SOME GENERAL REFERENCES

The books and journals devoted largely to evaluation research methods and to evaluation studies have multiplied considerably in the past two decades. Listed below are some of the major general references of which you should be aware, if you want to become knowledgeable about evaluation research theory and practice. The commentaries after each reference may be used as a guide to content.

A. Evaluation Journals

EVALUATION REVIEW: A Journal of Applied Social Research. (Formerly Evaluation Quarterly) edited by Freeman and Berk. Highly regarded as the best of the professional journals. Biased toward quantitative and formal approaches. Published bimonthly by Sage Publications. Interdisciplinary, often technical, and always of high quality.

EVALUATION NEWS. An official publication of the American Evaluation Association and formerly published by the Evaluation Network (see organizations, below). Published quarterly by Sage Publications. Contains mainly short articles addressed to professional issues and to substantive evaluation problems. Contains a useful set of short reviews of new publications in evaluation. Tends to favor more qualitative evaluation styles.

NEW DIRECTIONS FOR PROGRAM EVALUATION. Quarterly journal of The American Evaluation Association (formerly the Evaluation Research Society) and published by Jossey-Bass. Mainly special issues, some based on annual meetings of the society.

EVALUATION AND PROGRAM PLANNING. Independent quarterly specializing in evaluations of human services programs, especially mental health programs. Now officially the journal of the Eastern Evaluation Research Society, a regional affiliate of the American Evaluation Association.

EVALUATION STUDIES REVIEW ANNUAL. Annual collection of supposedly the best articles and unpublished pieces on evaluation methods and findings. Published by Sage Publications and edited by editors separately picked for each annual. Quality variable but some issues are extremely good.

POLICY ANALYSIS. Quarterly published by University of California Press and edited by Berkeley's public policy school. Largely devoted to policy analysis although there are many articles on evaluations.

JOURNAL OF POLICY ANALYSIS AND MANAGEMENT. Published quarterly by John Wiley and edited at Harvard's Kennedy School, this is about the best policy analysis journal going. Contains good reviews of recent literature.

B. **Sometime Evaluation Journals**:

These are journals in which evaluations and related policy research issues often appear, but not consistently.

HUMAN ORGANIZATION. Journal of the Society for Applied Anthropology.

SOCIAL PROBLEMS. Journal of the Society for the Scientific Study of Social Problems.

JOURNAL OF SOCIAL ISSUES. Journal of the Society for the Psychological Study of Social Problems (An affiliate of the American Psychological Association).

JOURNAL OF APPLIED PSYCHOLOGY. Although heavy on industrial psychology, occasional articles on evaluation appear.

JOURNAL OF HUMAN RESOURCES. Devoted largely to issues in labor economics and job training issues.

MEDICAL ANTHROPOLOGY. Devoted to cultural anthropology studies of medical problems and medical care.

HEALTH AND HUMAN BEHAVIOR. Published by the American Sociological Association and containing occasionally evaluation studies.

SOCIAL SCIENCE RESEARCH. Edited by James D. Wright, with many articles on evaluation issues and studies. Published by Academic Press.

In addition, from time to time, the mainline professional journals will publish articles on evaluation, especially on epistemological and technical issues.

C. Major General References On Evaluation

NOTE: IMPORTANT REFERENCES ARE MARKED WITH **.

Bennett, C. A., and A. A. Lumsdaine, **EVALUATION AND EXPERIMENTS**, New York, Academic Press, 1975. Excellent (although a little old) compilation of papers on field experiments evaluating innovative programs.

Berk, R. A., and P. H. Rossi, **THINKING ABOUT PROGRAM EVALUATION.** Newbury Park, CA, Sage Publications, 1990. An essay on some of the major problems to be encountered in impact assessment.

Campbell, D. T., and J. C. Stanley, **EXPERIMENTAL AND QUASI-EX-PERIMENTAL DESIGNS FOR RESEARCH, Skokie, IL, Rand McNally, 1966. A classic that has dominated the evaluation research design literature since publication. Concerned primarily with educational evaluations but very general in application.

Chen, H.-T., **THEORY-DRIVEN EVALUATIONS.** Newbury Park, CA. Sage Publications, 1990. A proposal for evaluations based on substantive theoretical models relevant to the subject matter being evaluated.

Cook, T. and D. T. Campbell **QUASI-EXPERIMENTATION DESIGN AND ANALYSIS ISSUES FOR FIELD SETTINGS**, Skokie, Il, Rand McNally, 1979. Excellent exposition of research designs used commonly in evaluations by two of the best practitioners of the art of exposition. Somewhat removed from practice, however.

Cronbach, L. J. (and associates), **TOWARD REFORM OF PROGRAM EVALUA-TION**, San Francisco, CA, Jossey-Bass, 1980. A founding father of the field and a large cast of associates at Stanford ruminate over its faults and suggest reforms in the form of 95 'theses'. Sensible suggestions although ponderously written.

Cronbach, L. J. **DESIGNING EVALUATIONS OF EDUCATIONAL AND SOCIAL PROGRAMS. San Francisco, CA, Jossey-Bass, 1982. An excellent new advanced text advancing a counter-Campbellian perspective that makes a great deal of sense.

Franklin, J. L. and J. H. Thrasher, **AN INTRODUCTION TO PROGRAM EVALUATION**, New York, John Wiley, 1976. An elementary introduction to program evaluation in the public health and health delivery fields.

General Accounting Office, **THE EVALUATION SYNTHESIS**. Program Evaluation and Methodology Division, Washington, DC, GAO, 1992. An exposition of the methods used by GAO in reviewing and synthesizing evaluations of various programs.

Guba, E. G., and Y. S. Lincoln, **EFFECTIVE EVALUATION**, San Francsico, CA, Jossey-Bass, 1981. Advocates of naturalistic, responsive evaluations. Perhaps the most enthusiastic advocates of qualitative approaches to evaluation.

Guttentag, M. and E. Struening (eds.), **HANDBOOK OF EVALUATION RESEARCH**, Newbury Park, CA, Sage Publications, 1975 (2 volumes). Although very much out of date, these two volumes are quite comprehensive in their coverage of major issues and substantive applications. Most of the chapter contributions (by quite well-known authors) were written in the late 1960s - just at the beginning of the flowering of the field.

Herman, J. L. (ed.), **PROGRAM EVALUATION KIT** (9 volumes). Newbury Park, CA, Sage Publications, 1988. (2nd Edition) A set of cookbooks written to help local agencies to carry out evaluation studies. Mainly oriented toward local educational agencies. Simply written and quite good, but not very sophisticated technically. Do not use on evaluations that count.

House, E. R., **EVALUATING WITH VALIDITY**. Newbury Park, CA, Sage Publications, 1982. Long essay on evaluations that can be used to improve programs, especially educational ones. Takes an anti-social-science viewpoint.

Judd, C. M., and D. S. Kenny, **ESTIMATING THE EFFECTS OF SOCIAL INTERVENTIONS, Cambridge, Cambridge University Press, 1981. An excellent survey of approaches to the quantitative assessment and estimation of net impacts of social programs.

McLaughlin, M. W., and Phillips, D. C. (eds.), **EVALUATION AND EDUCATION AT QUARTER CENTURY**. New York, National Society for the Study of Education, 1991. A set of essays by the giants in educational evaluation assessing the accomplishments of the last 25 years of educational evaluation.

Patton, M., **QUALITATIVE EVALUATION AND RESEARCH METHODS** (2nd Edition), Newbury Park, CA, Sage Publications, 1990. Strong advocacy of qualitative approaches, and very well reasoned.

Riecken, H., and R. Boruch (and associates), **SOCIAL EXPERIMENTATION**, New York, Academic Press, 1974. Outcome of an SSRC committee on social experimentation. Excellent and simply written review of the major issues (as understood in the early 1970s) in the design and conduct of large scale social experiments.

Rossi, P. H., and W. Williams, (eds.) **EVALUATING SOCIAL PROGRAMS**, New York, Academic Press, 1974. Outgrowth of a 1969 conference on evaluation. Excellent papers but out of date. Should be read out of antiquarian interest.

Scriven, M., **EVALUATION THESAURUS**, (3rd Ed.) 1977. Berkely, CA, Scarecrow Press (private press owned by Scriven). Scriven's views on evaluation given in the guise of a dictionary of evaluation terms. Written with grace and skill.

Scriven, M., **THE LOGIC OF EVALUATION**. Berkely CA, Scarecrow Press, 1980. An eccentric but very literate and amusing review of evaluation as an enterprise that must bend to fit the needs of the program being evaluated.

Shadish, W. R., T. D. Cook, and L. C. Leviton, **FOUNDATIONS OF PROGRAM EVALUATION: THEORIES OF PRACTICE. Newbury Park, CA, Sage Publications, 1991. A review of the major evaluation theorists and their writings, ranging from Campbell to Rossi. An excellent exposition of the major viewpoints on evaluation.

Suchman, E. A., **EVALUATION RESEARCH**, New York, Russell Sage, 1967. Old but very good. The best of the early comprehensive reviews of the field. Mainly addressed to public health field.

Smith, M. F., **EVALUABILITY ASSESSMENT: A PRACTICAL APPROACH.** Boston, MA. Kluwer Academic Publishers, 1989. A well written practical textbook on evaluability assessment.

Wachter, K. W., and M. L. Straf, (eds.) **THE FUTURE OF META-ANALYSIS**. New York, Russell Sage Foundation, 1990. An excellent collection of stellar papers on the future prospects of meta-analysis.

Wholey, J. S., **EVALUATION; PROMISE AND PERFORMANCE**, Washington, DC, The Urban Institute, 1979. Heavy emphases on program monitoring and evaluability assessments, especially of established programs. Can also be regarded as a do-it-yourself advocate.

Note: A few publishing houses -- Sage, Jossey-Bass, and Academic -- dominate the publication of evaluation-oriented books and texts. See their catalogues for long lists of general references in the field. Get on their mailing lists and you will never want for soporific reading when insomnia strikes.

D. Some Major Technical Reference Journals

JOURNAL OF THE AMERICAN STATISTICAL ASSOCIATION [JASA]. An excellent, diverse journal that contains an "applications" section which is especially of interest to evaluators and applied social scientists. Articles are often quite difficult.

JOURNAL OF THE ROYAL STATISTICAL SOCIETY. The British counterpart of JASA and very similar in content and style.

ECONOMETRICA. Journal of the Econometrics Society. Publishes articles on statistical issues, substantive problems and economic theory. Very useful (and often difficult) for the model building side of evaluation research.

JOURNAL OF ECONOMETRICS. Much like *Econometrica*.

PSYCHOMETRIKA. Journal of the Psychometric Society. Focuses on measurement issues. Often quite difficult.

BIOMETRIKA. Journal of the Biometric Society, publishing articles on statistical issues in the biological and health sciences. Often quite difficult.

BIOMETRICS. Much like *Biometrika*.

TECHNOMETRICS. Journal of the American Society for Quality Control. Publishes articles on statistical applications in the physical, chemical, and engineering fields. Has a lot of good materials for social scientists. Often very difficult.

JOURNAL OF EDUCATIONAL STATISTICS. Publishes articles on statistical applications in educational research.

SOCIOLOGICAL METHODOLOGY. Published by American Sociological Association. An annual volume of solicited and contributed pieces on methodological issues in sociological research. Uneven in quality and relevance to evaluation. Didactic and review articles are often quite good.

SOCIOLOGICAL METHODS AND RESEARCH. Quarterly devoted to sociological research issues. Currently struggling to fill each issue, and, as a result, quality is often marginal. There are, however, always some articles relevant to evaluation research.

E. Some General Technical References

These are books that contain expositions of the techniques used in many evaluation researches. Usually these also contain discussions of other techniques as well.

Achen, C., **THE STATISTICAL ANALYSIS OF QUASI-EXPERIMENTS.** Berkeley, CA, University of California Press, 1986. An excellent discussion of what are the appropriate statistical methods to apply to quasi-experiments. Read only in an optimistic mood.

Belsey, D. B. et al., **REGRESSION DIAGNOSTICS: IDENTIFYING INFLUENTIAL DATA AND SOURCES OF COLLINEARITY**, New York, John Wiley, 1980. An excellent discussion of some important things that can go wrong in multivariate analyses and some of the things you can do about it (sometimes).

Box, G. E. P. et al., **STATISTICS FOR EXPERIMENTERS**, New York, John Wiley, 1978. An integrated discussion of randomized experiments and analysis of variance in a very accessible form.

Box, G. E. P., and G. M. Jenkins, **TIME SERIES ANALYSIS FORECASTING AND CONTROL**, New York, Holden-Day, 1976. Still the best reference on modelling time series.

Chiang, A. C., **FUNDAMENTAL METHODS OF MATHEMATICAL ECONOMICS,** New York, McGraw Hill, 1974. An accessible and excellent reference for applied mathematics (e.g., calculus, matrix algebra) in the social sciences.

Cochran, W. C. **SAMPLING TECHNIQUES**, (3rd Ed.), New York, John Wiley, 1977. The classic text revised and still excellent. (This contains sampling theory.)

Cochran, W. C. **PLANNING AND EVALUATION OF OBSERVATIONAL STUDIES.** New York, Wiley-Interscience, 1983. Excellent discussion of non-experimental research procedures.

Cox, D. R., **PLANNING EXPERIMENTS**. New York, John Wiley, 1958. Still an excellent treatment of randomized experiments.

Dillman, D. A., **MAIL AND TELEPHONE SURVEYS: THE TOTAL DESIGN METHOD**. New York, John Wiley , 1978. A real cookbook for the conduct of mail and telephone surveys that get very high response rates. Especially good on mail surveys.

Freedman, D. A., **STATISTICS**, Cambridge, MA, Abt Books. 1980. Many argue that this is the best introduction to applied statistics around. Even seasoned researchers find it instructive. Very accessible.

Glass, G. V., B. McGaw, and M. L. Smith, **META-ANALYSIS IN SOCIAL RESEARCH**. Beverly Hills, CA, Sage Publications, 1981. Exposition of methods for aggregating and assessing the results of many evaluations. Somewhat out of date but a classic.

Groves. R. M., and R. L. Kahn, **SURVEYS BY TELEPHONE**, New York, Academic Press, 1980. Excellent discussion of random digit dialing methods of telephone surveys and their advantages. By two SRC survey experts.

Hanushek, E. A., and J. E. Jackson, **STATISTICAL METHODS FOR SOCIAL SCIENTISTS**, New York, Academic, 1978. A very good intermediate econometrics text with lots of examples from sociology and political science. Written for non-economists.

Harvey, A. C. **THE ECONOMETRIC ANALYSIS OF TIME SERIES**, New York, Halsted Press, 1981. Probably the best text on the analysis of time series from an econometric point of view.

Hoaglin, D. C. et al., **DATA FOR DECISIONS**, Cambirdge, MA, Abt Books, 1982. A good introduction to how data should be used to make policy decisions. Very accessible.

Judge, G. C. et al., **THE THEORY AND PRACTICE OF ECONOMETRICS**. New York, John Wiley, 1980. Perhaps the most wide ranging of the current econometrics texts. Many topics covered and covered well.

Kazdin, A. E., **SINGLE CASE RESEARCH DESIGNS: METHODS FOR CLINICAL AND APPLIED SETTINGS**. New York, Oxford University Press, 1982. Innovative attempt to quantify the study of single cases, mainly in clinical settings.

Kessler, R. C., and D. F. Greenberg, **LINEAR PANEL ANALYSIS, MODELS OF QUANTITATIVE CHANGE**, New York, Academic Press, 1981. All you might want to know about how to handle repeated measurements, primarily from surveys.

Kish, L., **SURVEY SAMPLING**. New York, John Wiley, 1965. An old, somewhat out--of-date, but excellent advanced text on the sampling of human populations.

Kish, L., **STATISTICAL DESIGNS FOR RESEARCH**. New York, John Wiley, 1987. Excellent discussions (although uneven) of experimental and quasi-experimental designs.

Lawless, J. K., **STATISTICAL MODELS FOR LIFETIME DATA**. New York, John Wiley, 1982. Everything you wanted to know about "life history" data and how to handle them.

Light, R. L. and D. P. Pillemer, **SUMMING UP: THE SCIENCE OF REVIEWING RESEARCH**. Cambridge, Harvard University Press. 1984. An excellent exposition of how to avoid biases in summarizing the results of many researches.

McCleary, R., and R. Hay, Jr., **APPLIED TIME SERIES ANALYSIS FOR THE SOCIAL SCIENCES**. Beverly Hills, CA, Sage Publications, 1980. A simple and straightforward elementary introduction to time series analyses.

Miles, M. and M. A. Huberman, **QUALITATIVE DATA ANALYSIS**. Newbury Park, CA, Sage Publications, 1984. An interesting discussion of how to treat qualitative data derived from "field work" in a rigorous way. Examples used are largely qualitative evaluations.

Mishan, E. J. **COST-BENEFIT ANALYSIS** (2nd Ed.). New York, Praeger, 1976. The full treatment. Very difficult without some background in economics.

Morrison, D., **MULTIVARIATE STATISTICAL METHODS** (2nd ed.), New York, McGraw Hill, 1976. An excellent intermediate text on multivariate statistical methods popular in education and psychology.

Pindyck. R. S., and D. L. Rubinfeld, **ECONOMETRIC MODELS AND ECONOMIC FORECASTS** (2nd ed.), New York, McGraw Hill, 1981. Perhaps the best intermediate text in econometrics with excellent treatments of simulations and univariate Box-Jenkins procedures.

Rossi, P. H., J. D. Wright, and A. B. Anderson, (eds.), **HANDBOOK OF SURVEY RESEARCH**, New York, Academic Press, 1983. A collection of fairly technical papers on sampling, survey questionnaire writing, measurement, and analysis problems in sample surveys. Not for the beginner, however.

Sudman, S., **APPLIED SAMPLING**, New York, Academic Press, 1976. An excellent introduction to population sampling from a practical perspective. (Not for persons looking for sampling theory.)

Sudman, S., and N. M. Bradburn, **ASKING QUESTIONS: A PRACTICAL GUIDE TO QUESTIONNAIRE DESIGN**. San Francisco, Jossey-Bass, 1982. Just what the title says it is. The best cookbook yet with plenty of examples.

Thompson, M. S., **BENEFIT COST ANALYSIS FOR PROGRAM EVALUATION**. Beverly Hills, CA, Sage Publications, 1980. A very accessible introduction to cost-benefit analysis used in evaluation of programs.

Tuma, N. B., and M. T. Hannan, **SOCIAL DYNAMICS: MODELS AND METHODS**. New York, Academic Press, 1984. An exposition of new methods for handling the analysis of change.

II: ORGANIZATION OF THE DISCIPLINE

A. Professional Societies (and sub-societies)

American Evaluation Association: This is the major professional society devoted to evaluation research. Formed in 1985, it is an amalgamation of the former Evaluation Research Society and the Evaluation Network. AEA holds its annual meeting in October or November. Publishes **New Directions in Evaluation** (quarterly: see above), **Evaluation News** (quarterly described above), and also sponsors monographs. Composed primarily of psychologists and sociologists and heavily oriented to human service social programs. Annual meetings are interesting, serious and small enough to enjoy. Membership about 2-3,000.

The AEA also has regional affiliates, such as the **Eastern Evaluation Research Society,** which also sponsor journals and annual meetings.

In addition, sections of the American Psychological Association, American Sociological Association, the American Economic Association, and the American Educational Research Association all have sessions at their annual meetings devoted to problems of evaluation.

B. Major Evaluation Research Producers

Evaluation research is now an industry with university departments, university research organizations, private firms with research branches, and private firms devoted mainly to evaluation all undertaking evaluation researches. In addition, some evaluation (perhaps a large proportion of all evaluations) is done within agencies with responsibilities for operating social programs.

However, as in other industries, there is considerable concentration. Although perhaps as many as 1,000-2,000 entities do evaluation research, as much as 50% of all the funds are obtained by the top 10-15 largest private firms, who do most of the large-scale (and expensive) evaluations. Some of the largest firms have more social science Ph.D.'s on their payrolls than most social science divisions within universities. For example, at its peak in the 1970s, Abt Associates had a staff of more than 100 Ph.D.'s and a support staff of about 400 research assistants and clerks.

Some of the largest firms are listed below:

Abt Associates, Inc. Cambridge, MA

The Rand Corporation, Santa Monica, CA (not-for profit)

Educational Testing Service, Princeton, NJ (not-for-profit)

Mathematica, Inc., Princeton, NJ

Manpower Development Research Corporation, NY (not-for-profit)

Battelle Memorial Institute, Columbus OH (not-for-profit)

The Urban Institute, Washington DC (not-for-profit)

Westat, Inc., Silver Springs, MD

Research Triangle Institute, Raleigh-Durham NC (not-for-profit)

National Analysts, Philadelphia PA

American Institutes of Research, Pittsburgh PA

A few of the major university affiliated research organizations that are also in the big league are as follows:

Institute for Research on Poverty, University of Wisconsin

NORC (National Opinion Research Center), University of Chicago

Institute for Social Research, University of Michigan

Survey Research Center, Temple University

In addition, most of the major graduate centers in the social sciences have one or more research centers in the social sciences that participate in evaluation research activities.

III: MAJOR SOURCES OF EVALUATION FUNDING ON NATIONAL LEVEL

Evaluations typically are funded by sponsors who have oversight responsibilities for the programs in question. On the national level this ordinarily means that federal departments and agencies are the sources of funds. Often Congress incorporates mandated evaluations into authorizing legislation, sometimes directing an agency to undertake an evaluation of a specific sort. National evaluations are typically funded by contract let to one of the major producers listed above.

The major federal agencies that frequently fund evaluations are:

Department of Education: Although its research budget has been literally decimated during the Reagan and Bush administrations, this department still conducts some of the major national evaluations. Currently it is planning for a national impact assessment of its vocational rehabilitation program. Tends to favor educational researchers as evaluators.

Department of Labor: Strong funder of evaluations concerned with its major manpower training, employment security (unemployment insurance, job placement), etc. Tends to favor economists.

Department of Agriculture: Funds evaluations in the fields of nutrition, food stamps, school lunch programs.

Department of Health and Human Resources: This humongous department funds evaluations mainly through its component agencies, among which the more prominent are: Public Health Service (includes National Institutes of Health, Center for Disease Control); Social Security Administration; Health Care Finance Administration; Federal Drug Administration, etc.

Department of Housing and Urban Development: Although also in eclipse as a research funding source during the Reagan-Bush regimes, HUD in the past has financed major social experiments and evaluations of many of its major programs.

Environmental Protection Agency: Currently concerned with the evaluation of its mass educational programs designed to raise public consciousness concerning hazardous substances.

Department of Defense: Runs major evaluations of human resources programs. Currently being forced by Congress into evaluations of its weapons systems.

General Accounting Office: Although it does not contract out its work, this agency has established an evaluation unit that undertakes evaluations at Congress' request. The Division of Program Evaluation Methodology now has about 50 Ph.D. level social scientists. The GAO reports, to be found in the government documents section of your library, are often excellent sources for publications of evaluations dealing with specific programs.

National Institute of Justice: A unit of the Department of Justice that has funded several field experiments on prospective criminal justice policies.

IV: SOME MAJOR EVALUATION RESEARCHES AND EXEMPLARY PUBLISHED MONOGRAPHS IN EVALUATION

Each of the books cited above as general reference books contain extensive bibliographies of evaluation studies. Many of the references are to so-called 'fugitive' documents (i.e. not distributed by major publishers nor published in easily accessible scholarly journals) and hence are difficult to locate in conventional university libraries. Some of the better ones that have been published in accessible form are listed below.

If you become stricken by a passion for evaluation, we suggest that you begin early to build your own library of fugitive documents. Build strong, deep shelves to hold them.

Many such documents, especially relating to studies that have been financed by federal agencies are available in microfilm xeroxed form through NTIS (National Technical Information Service) or ERIC (a computerized reference service supported by the Department of Education). **EVALUATION NEWS** (see journals above) contains a section on ongoing evaluation projects and recently issued reports.

A good university social science reference librarian can be of immense help in locating studies and arranging for access.

Although most evaluation researches or comments on evaluations are never published by commercial or university presses, some of the best ones and some of those that are concerned with major evaluation studies do get published. Listed below are some that we think are either excellent and/or concern major programs. The list has a bias and is incomplete.

Alkin, M. C. (Ed.), **DEBATES ON EVALUATION**. Newbury Park, CA, Sage Publications, 1990. Edited transcript of a conference held at Malibu in which leading evaluators -- Patton, Weiss, Conner, House, etc. wander through a discussion of their differences.

Berk, R. A. et al., **WATER SHORTAGE: LESSONS IN CONSERVATION FROM THE GREAT CALIFORNIA DROUGHT, 1967-1977**, Cambridge, MA, Abt Books, 1981. An analysis of the impact of water conservation programs on the consumption of water in California.

Blalock, A. B. (Ed.) **EVALUATING SOCIAL PROGRAMS AT THE STATE AND LOCAL LEVEL: The JTPA Evaluation Design Project.** Kalamazoo, MI, W. E. Upjohn Institute for Employment Research, 1990. Chapters describe the design of JTPA (Job Training Partnership Act) evaluation in the state of Washington. Quite detailed and complete.

Bradbury, K. L., and A. Downs, (eds.), **DO HOUSING ALLOWANCES WORK?** Washington, DC, Brookings Institution, 1981. Collection of essays evaluating the Housing Allowance Experiments conducted by Abt Associates and the Rand Corporation.

Bunker, J. P., B. A. Barnes, and F. Mosteller, **COSTS, RISKS AND BENEFITS OF SURGERY**. New York, Oxford University Press, 1977. A review of researches on the relative effectiveness of surgical versus non-invasive procedures, where there is a choice.

Cicirelli, V.G. et al., **THE IMPACT OF HEAD START**. Athens, OH, Westinghouse Learning Corporation and Ohio University, 1969. A very controversial first evaluation of one of the more prominent social programs for pre-school children.

Coleman, J. S. et al, **EQUALITY OF EDUCATIONAL OPPORTUNITY**. Washington, DC, Government Printing Office, 1966. A needs assessment research that radically changed the direction of educational research.

Coleman, J. S. et al, **HIGH SCHOOL ACHIEVEMENT: PUBLIC, CATHOLIC AND PRIVATE SCHOOLS COMPARED**, New York, Basic Books, 1982. A controversial attempt to assess the differential effectiveness of high schools, purportedly finding that the Catholic high school children achieve higher levels of math and verbal competence.

Conner, R., and C. R. Huff, **ATTORNEYS AS ACTIVISTS.** Beverly, Hills, CA, Sage Publications, 1979. Evaluation of program that subsidizes public interest lawyers.

Cook, T. **SESAME STREET REVISITED,** New York, Russell Sage Foundation, 1975. Classic critique of evaluation of famous children's educational TV program.

Cutright, P., and F. S. Jaffe, **IMPACT OF FAMILY PLANNING PROGRAMS ON FERTILITY: The U.S. Experience**. New York, Praeger, 1979. A brilliant use of demographic data and survey data to estimate the impact of family planning clinics in the US.

Davidson, D. et al., **EVALUATION STRATEGIES IN CRIMINAL JUSTICE,** Elmsford, NY, Pergamon, 1981. An account of the failure of an evaluation of juvenile justice programs in Michigan and a frank account of the sources of that failure.

Doolittle, F., and L. Trager, **IMPLEMENTING THE NATIONAL JTPA STUDY.** New York, NY. Manpower Demonstration Research Corporation, 1990. Description of the problems encountered in implementing a national randomized experimental design for the evaluation of Job Training Partnership Act programs.

Fairweather, G. W., and L. G. Tornatzky, **EXPERIMENTAL METHODS FOR SOCIAL POLICY RESEARCH**. Elmsford, NY, Pergamon, 1977. One of the best examples of the use of sophisticated evaluation research to design and refine a program for the successful reintegration into civilian life of persons discharged from mental hospitals.

Freeman, H., and I. Bernstein, I. **ACADEMIC AND BUREAUCRATIC RESEARCH**, New York, Russell Sage Foundation, 1975. Comparison of quality of evaluations undertaken by academic and non-academic researchers and funded by NIMH.

Friedman, D., and D. H. Weinberg, **THE ECONOMICS OF HOUSING VOUCHERS**, New York, Academic Press, 1982. Collection of papers on the Housing Allowance Experiments.

Gleser, G. C. et al., **PROLONGED PSYCHOSOCIAL EFFECTS OF DISASTER: A STUDY OF BUFFALO CREEK**, New York, Academic Press, 1981. An attempt by a group of social scientists to estimate the residual psychological effects of the Buffalo Creek disaster in which a dam burst wiped out a small West Virginia community. Extremely skillful.

Graham, J. D. (ed.), **PREVENTING AUTOMOBILE INJURY: NEW FINDINGS FROM EVALUATION RESEARCH.** Dover, MA, Auburn House, 1988. Series of reports on impact of seat belt, drinking, speed limit programs on automobile accident rates.

Gramlich, E. M. and P. P. Koshel, **EDUCATIONAL PERFORMANCE CONTRACTING: AN EVALUATION OF AN EXPERIMENT.** Washington, DC, Brookings Institution, 1975. A re-analysis of a pilot test of a program to contract out the teaching of certain subjects in high schools.

Kassebaum, G. et al., **PRISON TREATMENT AND PAROLE SURVIVAL**, New York, John Wiley, 1971. Classic controlled experiment evaluating the effectiveness of a group therapy program in California prisons. A good evaluation of a silly program.

Kelling, G. T. et al., **THE KANSAS CITY PATROL EXPERIMENT**, Washington, DC, The Police Foundation, 1974. Controlled field experiment on police patrolling strategies.

Kershaw, D., and J. Fair, **THE NEW JERSEY-PENNSYLVANIA INCOME MAINTENANCE EXPERIMENT**, New York, Academic Press, 1976. Narrative account of the first large scale income maintenance field controlled experiment.

McLaughlin, M., **EVALUATION AND REFORM: THE ELEMENTARY AND SECONDARY EDUCATION ACT OF 1965.** Lexington, MA, Ballinger, 1975. An account of the failure of attempts to evaluate the effectiveness of the impact of this federal legislation on the education of disadvantaged children.

Mielke, K.W., and Swinehart, J. W., **EVALUATION OF THE FEELING GOOD TELEVISION SERIES**. New York, Children's Television Workshop, 1977. A famous evaluation of an educational television program that led to the program being cancelled.

Milavsky, J. R., R. C. Kessler, H. C. Stipp, and W. S. Rubin, **TELEVISION AND AGGRESSION: A PANEL STUDY**. New York, Academic Press, 1982. An extremely skillful attempt to estimate the effects of watching violence on TV on the aggressive behavior of young school children,

Nathan, R. P. et al. **THE CONSEQUENCES OF CUTS**. Princeton, NJ, Urban and Regional Research Center, 1983. A qualitative attempt to assess the Reagan regime effects on local urban programs.

Peirce, W. S., **BUREAUCRATIC FAILURE AND PUBLIC EXPENDITURE**, New York, Academic Press, 1981. A review of the effectiveness of public programs of all sorts and the development of a theory for explaining why they fail.

Pressman, J. L., and A. S. Wildavsky, **IMPLEMENTATION.** Berkeley, CA, University of California Press, 1973. A description of how an important program was implemented improperly.

Raizen, S. A., and P. H. Rossi (eds.), **PROGRAM EVALUATION IN EDUCATION: WHEN? HOW? TO WHAT ENDS?** Washington, DC, National Academy Press, 1981. The report of a National Academy of Science Committee that reviewed the evaluation program of the Department of Education.

Rist, R. C. (ed.) **PROGRAM EVALUATION AND THE MANAGEMENT OF GOVERNMENT: PATTERNS AND PROSPECTS ACROSS EIGHT NATIONS.** New Brunswick, NJ, Transaction Publishers, 1990. Chapters describing evaluation activities in Canada, West Germany, Great Britain, the US, Denmark, Netherlands, Norway and Switzerland.

Robins, P. K. et al (eds), **A GUARANTEED ANNUAL INCOME: EVIDENCE FROM A SOCIAL EXPERIMENT**, New York, Academic Press, 1980. Reports on the income maintenance experiments conducted Seattle and Denver. Probably the best of the randomized field experiments of the 1970's.

Rossi, P. H., R. A. Berk, and K. Lenihan, **MONEY WORK AND CRIME: EXPERIMENTAL EVIDENCE**, New York, Academic Press, 1980. Report of a large scale randomized field experiment with persons released from the prisons of Texas and Georgia, the treatment being eligibility for unemployment compensation payments.

Rossi, P. H. and K. Lyall, **REFORMING SOCIAL WELFARE,** New York, Russell Sage Foundation, 1975. An assessment of the New Jersey Pennsylvania Income Maintenance Experiment.

Rossi, P. H., J. D. Wright, E. Weber-Burdin, and J. Pereira, **VICTIMS OF THE ENVIRONMENT: LOSSES FROM NATURAL HAZARDS IN THE UNITED STATES: 1970-1980**. New York, Plenum, 1983. A "needs assessment" of the losses suffered by households in the US over a decade, outlining the problems that are not affected by US natural hazards policies of relief.

Sherman, L., **EXPERIMENTAL INTERVENTIONS IN THE TREATMENT OF SPOUSE ABUSE**. Washington, DC, Police Foundation, 1980. A recent randomized controlled experiment testing police handling of spouse abuse complaints and the effectiveness of different approaches in reducing subsequent incidents of abuse.

Smith, M. L., G. V. Glass, and T. I. Miller, **THE BENEFITS OF PSYCHOTHERAPY: AN EVALUATION**. Baltimore, MD, The Johns Hopkins University Press, 1980. A meta-evaluation that summarizes and puts together several hundred evaluations of the effectiveness of psychotherapy.

Struyk, R. J. and M. Bendick, (eds), **HOUSING VOUCHERS FOR THE POOR**, Washington, DC, Urban Institute, 1981. Another set of articles summarizing the findings of the Housing Allowance Experiments run by Abt and Rand.

Vanecko, J. J. and B. Jacobs, **REPORTS FROM THE 100-CITY CAP EVALUATION: THE IMPACT OF THE COMMUNITY ACTION PROGRAM ON INSTITUTIONAL CHANGE**. Chicago, National Opinion Research Center, 1970. A description of the local community action programs financed by the federal government in the 1960s.

Williams, W., **GOVERNMENT BY AGENCY: LESSONS FROM THE SOCIAL PROGRAM GRANTS IN AID EXPERIENCE**, New York, Academic Press, 1980. A qualitative assessment of the impact of block grants on local programs.

Wilner, D.M., R. P. Walkely, T. C. Pinkerton, and M. Tayback, M. **THE HOUSING ENVIRONMENT AND FAMILY LIFE**. Baltimore, MD, Johns Hopkins University Press, 1962. A classic evaluation of the effects of public housing on households.

Wright, J. D. et al., **AFTER THE CLEAN-UP: THE LONG RANGE EFFECTS OF NATURAL DISASTERS**, Beverly Hills, Sage Publications 1979. An evaluation of the long range effects of natural hazard events (floods, hurricanes, and tornadoes) on growth trends in local communities.